no/sixteenths
poemsbymarkgudgel

With thanks to editors:
Kalee Olson and Jill Livingston

www.pfnbooks.com

no/sixteenths
Copyright © Mark Gudgel
2008 All rights reserved.

ISBN 978-0-578-00806-6

This book is fondly dedicated to
my students, who know that sneetches are sneetches.

With special thanks and appreciation to the Grandfather of the Amazing Baby Alex.

Table Of Concepts:

 Ten Arguments ....……………..p16
 This is the day……………………………..p25
 Inheritance..p27
 Breaking Bread……………………….....p33
 A Colored Stop Light…………………...p36
 The Hermeneutics of Coyote…………....p37
 Noah's Neighbor………………………..p40
 A Day's Perspective……………………..p42
 Quiet Summer's Afternoon……………..p45
 Tributes…………………………….......p47
 White Man is an Octopus……………....p49
 The Knife in my Garage………………..p51
 For Africa………………………………p53
 Art Deco God……………………………p56
 Hitler Arrived…………………………..p58
 Private Airplanes……………………….p60
 February 6..........…………………………p63
 Name and Rank………………………...p69
 America the Beautiful…………………. p77
 Let Me Tell You What I'm Made Of.....p79
 The Start of Something Good…….…… p81

 Bio & Reviews……………………….. p84

"I don't go so far as to think that the only good Indians are dead Indians, but I believe nine out of ten are, and I shouldn't inquire too closely into the case of the tenth."

    - Theodore Roosevelt
    26th President of the United States of America

Author's Preface:

The egregious crimes committed during the settlement of this great country may never be atoned for. The fact that the slaughter of innocent men, women and children, and the enslavement of entire races of people were the means by which the United States came into being, and that these crimes took place largely under a Christian flag, is a matter of tremendous shame to me both as a Christian and as an American. Christians have always been the worst representatives of Jesus Christ ever to walk the earth, and I fear that today, as millions upon millions of us turn our backs upon still more atrocities, from the suffering in Darfur to the homeless in our own home states, we continue to perpetrate the awful sin of indifference that has been from the beginning of our nation a horrible stain upon the very fiber of our existence. May God have mercy on us all.

These poems were written over a period of several years. Poetry is not a statement of doctrine, but an attempt to capture the very nature of a moment with only a meager pen and paper. The sentiments expressed within these poems are not necessarily the way I still feel about these issues today, but they chart a significant part of my journey, as I have grown and grappled with race, class, religion, politics, genocide, and the people of the world who I so badly want to love. I have lost friends over my Christian faith. I have occasionally lost faith over the actions of my Christian friends. In the end, I am, as we all are, a work in progress, a person still growing, still learning, still trying to come to grips with the world in which I live. I hope that what you find herein may help you in your own journey, and that discovering what I have gone through may lead you not astray, but closer to the light.

As I write this, I reflect upon this incredible day, this gift from a loving and benevolent God. It is a historic day. Today, Barrack Obama was sworn in as the 44th president of the United States of America, and, of course, the first African American president ever. I spent some of the day in prayer, and some of it in tears, as I know so many others did. In his inaugural address only a few hours ago, President Obama said something quite like this: "We can no longer afford indifference to the suffering outside our borders." I can only hope that for once, we have put in place a human being as our president who truly has the resolve and the integrity needed to stand up for what is right, and not for what is popular. In my students, I have always found hope. Today, I find it in the leader of the free world, and it gives me comfort, if only for a moment, to think that this man, Barack Hussein Obama, might truly be the change that this country and this world so desperately need. May God be with Him as he struggles. May God be with us all.

Mark R Gudgel

January 20, 2009

5:31 pm CST

no/sixteenths

"Ten Arguments for Racism"

I

1. South Dakota. "Black Hills" National Park is a billion-dollar industry of tourism, skiing, spelunking and gambling. Mostly gambling. Gambling with fate, with the future. Four enormous, dead white men preside over the hearing, as screaming children pet baby crocodiles and ride water slides down someone else's dreams. Somewhere else, an Indian picks commodity cheese off of his plate with a toothpick on the Rosebud reservation. On the Pine Ridge, another Indian dies from black mold.

2. Steven walks into his mother's apartment in Tucson. Steven knows she isn't there, but he needs her car. He takes it on drives, an old Chevy Malibu with rusted fenders and a bumper sticker reading "Trees Please" and another that says "I Love Cops" and he drives for miles, maybe years in his mind. He drives up the interstate to Winslow and there he stands on the corner, watching for a girl who will never come because he is an Indian, and this is not his state anymore. Silently, he climbs back into the car to drive north. If he doesn't stop on the reservation, he'll stop in Vancouver and see his cousin Mike. Maybe have a beer or something.

3. The New England Patriots won the Super Bowl for the eighth straight year. Bill Belicek was named president, and later king, because America loves football. America loves football so much that it

calls the national championship a world championship, and celebrates when cheaters win. It loves football so much it observes the Sabbath in the Fall and Winter months alone. It loves football so much that it has forgotten all about Jim Thorpe. America really loves football.

    4. The long-haired Indian woman who smokes too much and introduced me to Thomas King and Sherman Alexie became my friend in college. She helped me with my term papers. She helped me write letters to get me into grad school. She helped me understand myself. I hated her cigarettes, but I loved her. She was good to me, even though she didn't have to be, and I realized that this was uncommon, and I appreciated it even more.

    5. Steven's mother's car broke down in Utah. Two hundred years instructed Steven not to trust the Mormons to fix a Chevy Malibu. Steven spent four days walking out of Utah, north, toward Vancouver. He never put his thumb out and nobody ever stopped to ask why there was an Indian on the highway. Steven didn't need to tell them he didn't belong there. They already knew. The asphalt burnt the soles of his feet through his worn Converse All Stars. On the side of the road, Steven would pick up shards of obsidian and stare into the past, to the time when volcanoes were scary and white people were not. If Steven stared long enough, he found that he could see himself in the glassy surface of the obsidian, somewhere very near to here, in a place where he belonged.

6. At the middle school of my youth, we played football with the reservation schools. We feared the Indians, because they were tougher than leather. You couldn't hurt them. But our racism would not allow us to admit our fears. Mercilessly we yanked on the long, majestic ponytails that flowed from underneath their battle-scarred helmets.

7. I didn't get in to the American Indian Studies department at Tucson. They "lost" my application. When I told them where to find it, it was too late. My long-haired Indian friend who smokes too much had to explain to me that there were other reasons, reasons with more history behind them. When I finally started to understand, we laughed together. It was refreshing to be discriminated against, for once. I am certain that when it is more frequent, it is less amusing, but my white self found it funny that day, even though it meant I had to get a job. I had a cigarette with her, and after that she left.

8. It was a few months later. I e-mailed my long-haired Indian friend who still smokes too much to e-tell her that I had gotten into a different school. I was teaching, and I would get a graduate degree in Biblical theology. It was days before I heard back. When I did, she e-told me to kill myself, accused me of wanting to steal her soul. She attacked my religion and my skin and she attacked my heart, my intellect. This time, I did not laugh.

9. Steven stopped in Spokane to call his mother. She was at home playing pinocle with some friends from the YWCA. Steven apologized for

stealing her car and for leaving it in Utah at the mercy of the Mormons. She asked him if he needed anything and he said yes. He said he needed her to tell him one more time about his place in the world, about how his people were mighty in the eyes of God. Steven's mother read him his favorite Iktomi story over the telephone as her friends continued playing cards. In his mind, Steven pictured the colorful illustrations of the book, imagined holding his own tattered copy in his hands, the one his mother was reading from. In his mind he could feel the blunt edge of the cover, and where it frayed in the place he had spilled apple juice on it when he was four. The pages were wrinkled, and the book was heavy in his lap, as it had been in his youth. When she finished reading, Steven thanked his mother and she went back to the card game. He hung up the payphone and stepped out into the Washington rain, ready again to face the world, if only for another evening. And the rain came down.

    10. I guess that she was remembering the boarding schools and the small pox blankets. I guess that she was remembering driving into the white town to get groceries to take back to the reservation as a little girl. I guess she was thinking about class field trips to Mount Rushmore, getting paddled by priests for being a savage, curfews and dresses that made her look funny. I guess she was remembering Sand Creek. I guess those things never really go away, even if you want them to, or think that they might. I guess time doesn't heal every wound. I guess it didn't

heal hers. I know it hasn't healed mine. I guess that maybe nothing ever will.

II

First:
  Japan and the rape of Nanking
Second:
  Nazi Germany and the Holocaust
Third:
  The Khmer Rouge and 1.7 million Cambodian souls
Fourth:
  The Interhamwe and Rwanda
Fifth:
  America and the Sand Creek Massacre
Sixth:
  America and the Trail of Tears
Seventh:
  America and boarding schools
Eighth:
  America and me
Ninth:
  America and you
Tenth:
  America and everything that comes after us

III

One:
Thou shall have no other gods before me.
Not the god of gold or the god of death,
not the god that hates the vast unknown.
Not the god of greed, the greed that meant
the end of a nation, the end of a people.

Two:
Thou shall not make for thyself an idol.
Nor shall thou become one, thought the
Lord. But we did. We made ourselves
the gods of the new world, and ruled it
with a murderous iron fist, and with greed.

Three:
Thou shall not misuse the name of the Lord.
Conquering, killing, stealing, all in the name
of Spain, in the name of the Holy Roman
Catholic church. Whose name then, was to
be misused? Whose name was taken in vain?

Four:
Thou shall observe the Sabbath day, keep it
holy. But the killing did not end, not on the
Sabbath day or on any other day. The rape
and the malice were never given leave, as the
god of war and greed was never to grow tired.

Five:
Thou shall honor thy mother and thy father.
But what, O God, of thy Father above? What
spoils of the earth could be offered to appease
Your wrath upon seeing what was done? Surely,
mothers and fathers shall weep with us in Hell.

Six:
Thou shall not murder. But murder, so singular
a term, does not do justice to the genocide that
took place, that takes place. Are blankets infected
with smallpox murder, or is it something for which,
My God, You never even dreamed a name?

Seven:
Thou shall not commit adultery. But what,
O God, of our unadulterated hatred for those
who came before us? What of the respect Your
people have never had for one another, nor for
You in their wanton quest to adulterate a world?

Eight:
Thou shall not steal. The land belonged to
no one, because the land belonged to every
one. Now the land, from the coasts to the
Paha Sapa to the Meccas to the plains is
counted by the acre, and stolen from the earth.

Nine:
Thou shall not give false testimony against
your neighbor. O Lord, then what testimony

can be given for a neighbor, about whom all
the truth is damning, about whom little can be
said except, perhaps for that he is one of us?

      Ten:
Thou shall not covet thy neighbor's wife.
But why, O Lord, should she be the only thing
upon the earth that we do not murder one another
for? Why not the neighbor's wife, if the very path
she walks is to be stolen from underneath her?

"This is the day"

"This is the day that the Lord has made,
      let us make noise and be fat in it."

If you look over there, deeper, just
past the horizon down Route 66,
you can almost see the people there
who beat you to the spot.

Still they are running.

My People
came to take My Country away
from My Friends and to hide
their crimes behind My God.

My God, this is all My Fault.

"This is the day Gerald Ford has made,
      let us rejoice and be glad in it."

You can learn a lot about a person by
spending time with them, but you learn
even more when they refuse to spend
their time with you.

My skin tone is My Yellow Star.

At night, I can curl up in my soft white
blankets and cry out for forgiveness; at

night, I can see in my dreams Borglum's
monster coming down.

"This is the day that the Lord has made,
        let us rejoice and be glad, enit?"

How little do we understand, to believe
that redemption can occur at the end
of a smoking barrel, to continue to delude
ourselves that separate can be equal.

Separate is what happens when equal does not.

I want the world to know that Colonol
Chivington burns in Hell; I want to force
white Christian children into boarding schools
and with them at the top of our lungs cry out:

"This is the day that the Lord has made,
        let us rejoice and be glad in it!"

"Inheritance"

Her inferiority was born in the driver's seat of a 1973 Pontiac convertible, the one her father gave her. It was a single-tone faded light blue on the outside, with galaxy-shaped patches of rust showing through all over like small islands in a tropical sea. Her interior of cracked white leather smelled of pine needles and must, though most days, it held her up just fine. The car had been a gift, and one she cherished greatly, though more for the sentiment than for its value. While she didn't mind at all the sub-cherry appearance of the behemoth, the mechanical parts of the car never seemed to be working right. At least not at the same time. She would finally save enough money to fix the transmission, and the brakes would fail. Or she would fix the tail-lights, like the sheriff told her to, and just as she did, the high beams would go out. Still, most days she would drive the monster the eleven miles it was between her front door and the high school, praying all the way that "ol bess" would get her there just one more time, or back home, Lord please just one more time. But the unpredictable Midwestern weather and the holes in the canvas top continued to wear away on her, until at last one day she came out of school to find all four tires crumpled underneath the gray steel rims as though they had been run over by themselves. It began to rain at mile four, and by mile nine she had concluded, without consulting her alcoholic father, nor calling her mother who she could probably reach at the "Double T" saloon two states away, that she would take a week off from school, work, and try to save up enough money to buy four more tires for that 1973 Pontiac convertible, the one her father gave her.

The week became a month, became a term, and then a year. That would have been her junior year in high school, had she remained. But she liked the money, and working in the local café for tips, she never had to fix the car, or study Spanish, or learn math or read books she hated about the conquests of white people over the past two thousand years. She could simply work, and for a while, she enjoyed life that way. A pleasant routine, simple, without the bothers of noisy cities, pressures to compete, earn grades, never quite being the best at anything, so never recognized at school, never quite recognizable at home. Work was a way to forget about all that, and so she worked, and she worked hard, and that old 1973 Pontiac convertible, the one her father gave her, sat behind the double-wide with its four flat tires, the rust islands growing as the sea of light blue paint receded back further and further away from them, finally giving way to an inevitable return to the earth. When her father's liver finally died, he went along with it. Some of her co-workers mused behind her back that there was no point in him sticking around without it, but of course, they never said such things directly to her. For a time, she would cry dutifully whenever anyone would mention him, though eventually she decided it was time to give that up. She had not seen her mother in years, and when she tried the "Double T" saloon two states away, the muffled laughter on the other end confirmed what she had suspected for some time. The Army paid for her father's funeral, but the pension checks stopped coming, and eventually she learned that the double-wide did not belong to her father, but to the bank, and that they wanted it back now. She could hardly argue, so she packed her few things into the suitcase that her mother never used, climbed into the 1973 Pontiac convertible, the one her father gave her, and drove with four flat tires the three miles to the mechanic, where he charged her everything she had inherited to fix her rims and put new tires on the behemoth, the one her father gave her, which again needed new tail lights, and also, now, a radiator.

For years she worked and worked at the café, sleeping on couches and in basements, sometimes dating older men just so that she might have a place to sleep at night. Eventually, she began to realize why her father had become an alcoholic, and why he never went to work and why he used to beat her mother until she finally left one day. It occurred to her that she would never have the life that she had wanted for herself, that perhaps it was impossible. That there was some Divine or cosmic force that did not want her to succeed in the manner in which her society now gauged success. She would never be wealthy, she would never have family the way she saw it on television. She was what she had always been told she would be, she had lived up to the potential that her teachers and her classmates and her society had seen reflected in the dark color of her skin, stretched taut across the muscles that were no longer strong enough to lift her back up off the ground. When she realized this, she didn't say a word, merely hung her apron on a hook in the café kitchen and stepped out into the rain. She drove the 1973 Pontiac convertible, the one her father gave her, two counties over, where she found a used car dealer who offered her five hundred dollars and half a bottle of whisky for it. She gladly accepted, walked over to the street corner where an awning shielded her from the rain, uncorked her father's favorite and only passtime, and drunk deep the recognition of her life's work in a bottle.

Five months passed, which she spent getting acquainted with the various people of the town, most of whom tolerated her nonviolently and knew her as "that woman." The five hundred dollars had lasted only long enough for her to get addicted to the whisky and whatever passable substitutes she could find, and she spent as many nights working on her corner as she did drinking on it. The men at the local bar knew always where to find her, and most of them knew what kind of whisky she preferred. As the rain turned into snow and the heat to cool and then to bitter cold, she began breaking into garages to shield her from the weather, in the hopes that there may be money, other valuables, occasionally even booze, knowing that with luck she might be arrested again, and get to spend a few nights in the heated jail eating tuna fish sandwiches on white bread with Ready Whip. She really liked Ready Whip, and whisky, and heat. Two of those she could get in jail.

Then one day in early January, though she didn't know it was, she broke into a garage, part of her usual routine, and there, underneath a tarp parked next to the bass trawler, was her car, her beautifully restored 1973 Pontiac convertible, the one she sold for five hundred dollars and half a bottle of whisky. It had been purchased by the county attorney, and given to his son on his sixteenth birthday. No longer did the rusty islands linger and expand along the long, sleek body of the car. The sea of perfect light blue flowed waxy and unblemished. The top had been replaced, and the taillights as well. As she ran her hands along the shiny frame, she could scarcely believe that such a fine thing had once belonged to her. But she knew that it was hers as she peered inside the perfect glass windows. The attorney's boy had not yet had the time to replace the cracked white leather of the car's interior. The front seats wore seat covers that said "bad to the bone," and in the back, the boy's schoolbooks lay scattered on the seat and floor. With a tear in each of her silent eyes, she forced the passenger side door of that 1973 Pontiac convertible, the one her father gave her, and climbed gently into the back seat, laying herself across the cracked white leather, being careful not to disturb the young boy's schoolbooks, and finally giving way to an inevitable return to the earth.

"Breaking Bread"

Every Indian I ever met was drunk. Except
I never really met them. I just
looked at them as we walked by;
I didn't get it. "Why don't they just stop
drinking," I'd ask my mother, who would
always make her answer something like
"Some people just make bad decisions."

I remembered that in college when I
got a D.U.I.;
the officer holding me at gun point
after I had attempted to explain to her
that some people just make mistakes.
She didn't seem to realize in the dark
that I was white, or maybe she just
didn't care.

The difference between the Indians of
my childhood and myself was not the
color of our skin, but the richness of
our opportunities.

I learned about commodities working
in a grocery store, and hearing white
people complain.

I learned about HUD houses in college,
from an Indian who got paid a lot for having
once have lived in one, and for her Ph.D.

I never came home to a meal of commodity
cheese and soda crackers, or had one of those
HUD houses fall in on me.

I learned that Indians drink too much by
observing it, by being told over and over again
that that was the difference between them
and us.

I drank too much just to prove them wrong.

In December, in Valentine, Indians move
about to keep warm. While everything else
is still and frozen, you can see them, scarcely
moving in the shadows of the moon.

On Christmas eve, my father, who has
never believed in Jesus, took a walk
with me to the gas station. On our way
in, one of those shadows asked us for
some money.

According to the clerk at the gas station,
he was drunk, just like all the rest
of them.

On the way out, my father handed Him
a huge yellow bag of Lays potato chips,
extra crispy, low in saturated fats.

That Christmas eve night, I learned what
it means to be grateful; I finally met somebody
who actually was. And he and my father
shared a potato chip together.

I don't head back to Valentine
often. To me, the ugly outweighs
the good and the bad. Though I never
forget that night, that frigid dark night,
two thousand years and a day before we
celebrate the birth of Christ, when my
Father broke bread with an Indian, and
in front of His only begotten son, He
fed 4000 more.

"A Colored Stop Light"

Red.

And I glance over fast;
she must be purt-near ninety
so I look away.

She didn't see me, and I'm curious,
so I look again.

Yep, she's ninety-ish. And I can't tell if
she's Indian-Indian or American Indian,
or maybe Mexican. Her wrinkles and
my fear of making eye-contact with her
keep me from finding out. Those things
keep me even from rolling down
my window and saying hi. They prevent
us from getting to know one another,
even from sharing a smile.

Fear defines my people.

Green.

And off I go.

"The Hermeneutics of Coyote"

    "Hey," said Coyote to Pterodactyl,
    "You should really try the apples."
    "Already have," replied Pterodactyl.
    "They're delicious."
    "Yes," said Coyote.
    "And you're naked," said Pterodactyl.
    "I suppose I am," said Coyote.

The next day, Coyote came again to Pterodactyl.

    "Hey," said Coyote to Pterodactyl,
    "Do you know what would be funny?"
(Coyote always knows what will be funny)
    "You should tell those new guys to
eat one of our delicious apples. Then they will
know that they are naked and we can sell them
our fur to cover up with."
    "I don't have any fur," said Pterodactyl.
    "It's okay," said Coyote. "We'll just
sell them mine."
    "That's very generous of you," said
Pterodactyl.
    "Yes, it is," said Coyote.

The next day, Pterodactyl approached First Woman.

    "Did God really say, 'You must not
eat from any tree in the garden'?" asked Pterodactyl.
    "Yep," said First Woman. "He said we could

eat from any tree but the one in the middle, and that if we did, we would surely die."

"You will not surely die," said Pterodactyl.

"In fact," said Coyote, who had crept in through the back door, "You will be like Him."

"I could be like God?" asked First Woman.

"Yep," said Coyote.

"All you have to do is eat the yummy apples and you can be just like God," said Pterodactyl. He was having fun now. "You might even get wings like me."

First Woman went back to the first dwelling to discuss things with First Unfaithful Drunkard. He wanted to fly, so they decided to eat the apples.

Stuff really hit the fan after that. First Unfaithful Drunkard tried to blame First Woman, but God only got more angry for his lies. First Woman, who has always been slightly more clever than her counterpart, as a general rule, blamed Pterodactyl, which
was partly true.

Then God said to Pterodactyl, "Cursed are you above all the livestock and all the wild animals. You will
crawl on your belly and you will eat dust all the days of
your life."

Then He took away Pterodactyl's wings and He took away his legs. Pterodactyl slithered over to First Woman and hissed at her. She jumped up on a chair and screamed until First Unfaithful Drunkard hurled a bottle in his general direction, and then he slithered off.

"Hoooo-boy!" said Moses many years later.
"They'll never be able to understand any of this."
"I have an idea," said Coyote.

"Noah's Neighbor"

Noah's neighbor
surely looked upon him with the
suspicion of a stray cat, staring
in the window. I get up, excited
to pet him and he flees into
the darkness.

But later he is back.

Noah's neighbor
could not have helped but to
stare curious into the window of
my living room at the insatiable
labors of that ancient man
from Sinai.

Why is he doing that?

The cat, I know, is hungry,
but having been betrayed by
people in the past, will not risk
his fur-covered neck over what
I only might have to give
to him.

As God looked on, solemn, sober.

Noah's neighbor
surely knew long in advance

that this coming rain would be
the last his world would see. Surely
recognized the boat. Surely tried to
buy a ticket.

And cats have always hated water.

"A Day's Perspective"

Wake up. In the grog of morning, as you stumble over your shoes, pants, Bible, realize that not everybody did.

Arrive at work and complain about hating everything about it. Then spend your paycheck frivolously on corn chips, beer, gasoline and cigarettes.

(Note the homeless man outside your window as you're driving home.)

Teach a lesson on tolerance. Be informed by a junior in high-school, and a cheer captain, no less, that you yourself are intolerant towards racists, bigots, anti-Semites, and all other array of scum. Agree with an embarrassed smile. Move on to the Civil War.

Be present during a presentation on the Holocaust. Asked to step into a taped-out train car on the floor of the gym (please do) begin to feel claustrophobic in those close-if-wall-free quarters. Feel relief at the sound of the school bell, step out, learn nothing. Nod to the fellow in charge as you walk away, applaud his valiant effort while wincing at the damage he has done to empathy.

Teach a lesson on Bosnia. Afterward, have a student approach you professing to be a Bosnian. Listen in horror as he tells you that his uncle was flayed alive as he himself watched helplessly from just inside the forest. Share a tear and a handshake, and feel that your lesson has done a disservice to humanity. Know that he agrees with you. Tomorrow you will teach about something that is safer, something that matters much, much less.

Remark upon the understanding that, at a job you know you suck at, it was a particularly bad day.

Have a piece of cold pizza. Taste bodies. Rinse it down with a couple fingers of cheap gin.

Arrive late to your tenure class and interrupt the session. Sit down, apologetically of course, and breathe gin on the hapless married woman seated across the tiny table from you. Smile a roguish smile, and be revealed to be as pathetic as you are fast becoming.

Walk into the bathroom of Kahoa elementary during break. Recall that you do not recall the urinals being so short. Remember a time when pissing in them did not hurt your knees or make a mess.

Drive home sadly and, while cutting off an old woman in a Cadillac, remember flipping off the young woman who did the same to you but moments prior. Recognize that the number of people now in your life whom you desperately want to tell to screw their furriest pet is directly proportionate to the number of people who would likely request that you be tarred and feathered for the most recent breath you took. Remember how much you hated math class.

Ignore phone calls from your friends as you selfishly seek to advance your own career. Feel regret, but do not return their calls. Do make mental plans to send Christmas cards in February. Know inside that you will fail to do even that.

Microwave a stove-top box while thinking to yourself that you are starving. Realize later that it was your Bosnian student, and not you, who might ever have known the meaning of the word. Correct yourself. You are hungry.

You are always hungry.

"Quiet Summer's Afternoon"

Finished working on your tan, you
Say goodbye to your friend who brought
The football to the pool at your apartment
Complex and step into the air-conditioned
Comfort of your tiny living room.

Exhausted from inactivity and being obli
gated to nothing on this day, you pick up
Your new copy of *All that is not Given is
Lost* and your new Anthony Julius book
Confirming the awful truth about T.S. Eliot
Which you had secretly perhaps always
Suspected.

You ask yourself why everyone hates the
Jews, or better, why everyone thinks that
Everyone hates the Jews. You think to
Yourself that you certainly don't hate any
Jews. As your mind begins to calm itself,
You climb into the sink, emerging with a
Dirty coffee cup from the day before when
You had company. Not bothering to rinse
It out, you reflect upon the conversation you
Had had with your company, specifically
The one about the national deficit reaching
Eight trillion dollars, and you fill the brown-
Stained mug with a few fingers of honeyed
Whisky and a couple cubes of ice. Unplug
The telephone.

You sit on the deck in the heat of the after
Noon, happily shaded by the cottonwoods
On the north end of the house, and you begin
To read poetry. Out loud. From time to time
You pause, stare bleakly down into your mug
Of thought and broken homes, a mug much
Better suited for holding coffee, in a hand
Much better suited for writing, for opening
Doors and brushing teeth. You watch as the
Iridescent swirls of freezing honeyed liquor
Dance around the ice cubes, flowing and
Whispy, like magic, like dirt.

You drink, and in an instant, wonder if
Your children will ever pay off that debt, and
Whether or not your new tan will have any
Thing to do with when you have those child
Ren, and why people so often allow thems
Elves to become so attached to one anoth
Er, and to whisky, especially the kind wit
H honey in it, and then, in quiet desperat
Ion, you drop your books and your old coff
Ee mug, and with a backwards glance towar
D the swimming pool from whence you c
Ame, you fly to your desk in a rustle of fe
Athers and emotion, lift your pen, and beg
In to write it all down, in the solemn lonel
Y hope that someday, it will be read and m
Ade good sense of.

"Tributes"

They just erected another huge building in Omaha, Nebraska. It's one of those rare skyscrapers on the plains that isn't a grain elevator. I drove past it the other night, huge and glowing, greater and more expensive than any wigwam ever built.

Omaha. I have a hard time thinking that my society still calls a city by the name of an Indian tribe. As though it were some sort of brutish tribute. Maybe once we've finished leveling Iraq, we can name it something fitting like that.

We could call it Sunni. Or we could call it Dick Cheney. Who would object? Let's just call it Dick.

But there are so many other tributes like this one. Omaha is a great city, you could argue, the biggest in the state, and thus a fitting tribute.

But what about Ogallala? It isn't even spelled right, and the dying town on the Western plains exists only because it's on the road to Denver, which was named after their professional basketball team.

But the Oglala are also on the road to Cheyenne, named for the Cheyenne Indians. Cheyenne is the biggest city in Wyoming, so maybe that one's okay. At least for now.

Back in Nebraska, there's Winnebago. I don't think most folks outside the town know that it's an Indian name. They think the town is named for the RVs some Indians live in, or for the casino.

There are so many more; Spokanne, and so on. Some of them are great cities, as great as a city can be I suppose. Some of them are miniscule dots on the map, or dots that don't even make the map because no white person would ever drive there. Whatever they may be, it's ugly to name things after the people you stole them from.

Somewhere out there, somebody is riding a bike named "David" or wearing a skirt they call "Herberger's." That seems to be the American way, and if it helps a country to get to sleep at night, then maybe it's necessary.

But maybe not.

"White Man is an Octopus"

There is a white man
in each of us. Some wear him on the
outside, like me; he is half freckle,
half overcoat. He lurks in the depths
like an octopus underneath a barge,
glaring up coldly at the well-lit world,
the unwitting passers-by, contemplating
what next he can steal away into his
murky lair.

Indians have a white man in them, too
(forgive me, please, it is my overcoat
speaking) though he lurks inside, where
even the divers can not see him, where
even the missionaries failed to look. He
is a trickster and a drunk, and some nights,
he'll let you know just that, as he coolly
convinces you to have just one more.

Black people have a white man, too. They
call him "bling" and they wear him like a
parrot on their shoulder, a witless conversation
piece. "See my white man?" they say to one
another, understanding all the while that the
white man is merely symbolic of their loss, and
that most of us are made out of cubic zirconium
anyway.

I am a white man, and an octopus is crushing my heart. When I can subdue him with alcohol, he pleads with me to give back the Paha Sapa, and to become a warrior, to do battle for what he insists I know is right. But when I can not subdue my white octopus, he rages within me, no longer just a metaphor. He grows stronger with every passing of another unjust sunset in America, and I pray for the day when he will release us all.

"The Knife in my Garage"

That old sword from the Indian wars, the
one I bought in Denver from the man selling
jewelry; I like to pretend that it belonged to
Colonel Chivington, and that it fell from his
bleeding hands at Sand Creek when he
ran cowardly away from great Indian warriors
with great red bows loaded with great red
arrows, all of them poised to fly into his heart.

I hold the sword, tarnished and ancient, shiny
on the tip where someone clumsily attempted
to give it a double edge. I like to think about
his children, daughters no doubt, who sat in
the pew on Sunday listening to daddy thump
away at the pulpit, believing every savage,
twisted word he ever uttered about the God
he never knew. I think of them, with long
blonde hair, laying in the sun on a Saturday
afternoon in July, the hot Midwestern sun
slowly turning their skin darker, into red.
Their tan line the mark of their malcontent, a
criss-cross in triple sixes, daddy killed them
in their sleep.

The Cheyenne have never approached me
about giving them the sword, though I suppose
they ought to have it. The blood of Black Kettle's
people mingling on the graying blade with that
of the Methodist monster's daughters, their

screams crying out in harmony, as together they descend. "Father, father, why have you forsaken me?"

"For Africa"
After "The Raven" by Edgar Allen Poe

Once upon a forgotten plain,
scorched by the sun and soaked in rain,
in a land so far away that the world
had forgotten it was ever there –
Shots rang out in all directions,
grass huts offered no protection,
and man could muster no affection,
man claimed not to be aware.
Bodies fell and blood ran thick,
while we claimed not to be aware –
It's awful, yes, but over there.

A hatred that had brewed for years
so quickly turned itself to tears
as machetes brought to life their fears and
through their heavy flesh did tear –
The wretched fled in all directions,
from where the French and Belgians left them,
no place offered them protection,
corpses with their backs so bare.
Bodies piled with no protection,
corpses with their backs so bare –
Too far away for us to care.

On the Western news they're saying
that the reason for their acts delaying
is that all of us stopped praying,

stopped praying to our God so fair.
Godless we without affection,
for our fellow man's protection,
unless of course there's an election
to make a man pretend to care –
Yes candidates in the election
do indeed pretend to care –
about the wretched over there.

One conflict ends, another starts,
in countries not so far apart
as we can't see it in our hearts
to intervene, not over there –
For us there is no clear connection,
why should we offer protection
when the section of the world
with oil isn't over there?
The section of the world that has
our oil isn't over there –
But for what other reasons might we care?

And so the blood continues spilling
as the world continues killing
children, we seem all too willing,
to let them die – not being there.
As we await the resurrection,
death arrives for dark complexioned
persons who without affection
concede to death, we know not where.
These people who have no affection,

folks for whom we never care –
So awful, yes, far over there.

And once again with sirens blaring,
the world arrives too late for sparing
even one life for which caring
earlier may have saved them there –
Still years into our interjection
we may stop, make a connection
and in our minds a brief reflection
about what we could have done there –
As pulpit pounding monsters deliver
tired lines we've heard before –
Oh yes, we've heard these tired lines
a thousand times before.

Yet quoth the world "Nevermore."

"Art Deco God"

I have never been able to kneel down
to pray
or worship with any level of comfort in
any of those huge stone churches put up
in the middle of last century. The Roman
Catholics did it, the Methodists, even
the Presbyterians built them; huge
and sandstone, with enormous worship
chambers, extra-long wooden pews,
out of place steel and glass doors and
as much stained glass as they could afford at
the time. And in these churches,
every one I've ever seen, there is always
amongst the mess and congregation
one great, enormous, Aryan Jesus looking
down upon His people. I hate that
Jesus, the One that man created, the One that
isn't real.

Jesus is real, but He isn't
the artist's rendition, the artist who ran out
of color and had to resort
to the white left on his palate. The Real
Artist didn't ever run out, and Jesus
isn't as cursed white as the Hitlers of the
Protestant Reich want us all to think.

Jesus is alive and well, He's real and they say
He'll be back soon. And if you believe that, you
should probably say your prayers tonight,
because the Lord will undoubtedly be a little
miffed that we have subtracted all the color from
His holy face.

"Hitler Arrived"

Hitler arrived in America
in 1492.

He shook their hands before
he cursed them into dog-birds.

He took their lands and their
freedom;
he never looked back.

When he had enough power and
enough army, he forced them
into crowded concentration camps
and ordered their death.

Hitler invaded the holy lands
and raped them of their beauty
and their quiet.
He desecrated sacred temples
and carved his faces in their stones.

Hitler stole the trees and the gold,
he took from each of them their lands,
their futures, their hopes;
he took from each of them their pride,
replacing it with bottles empty like promises,
with HUD houses surrounded by ugly
tangles of barbed-wire, guards and dogs.

Hitler pursued and executed their leaders,
as many as he could.
Those he couldn't kill he had imprisoned
in Leavenworth, Kansas.

450 years later, Christopher
Columbus seized Germany, trained the
American Youth and the Schutzstaffel,
started World War II, and
to this day I am in awe of having
never met a Jewish Indian.

"Private Airplanes"

When I was little, much
younger than I am now, I used to
love to take the musty beaded lawn-
chairs from our mossy, wooden
deck (though my mother asked
me not to) and I would make them
be my private airplanes.

I would flip one over, they were
so light, and rest the bumpy-beaded
seat atop my soft, young skull, my
hands upon the handles, turned upside
down. The armrests became windows
and I would buzz through the yard
across the street and over the neighborhood
houses, high above the catalpas
in my private airplane.

Today I sat back in my padded
office chair as my ninth graders
diligently took in notadamnthing about
Indians. The bell rang and they
all departed routinely for the
soccer fields, for their Nintendo
games, not realizing that back home,
not far from where I used to fly, there
were people whose soccer fields
are filled with broken glass, scattered
with rusty nails, with tears, with shame.

They left not realizing that not everybody
has an X-box on which to slay dragons,
to save busty princesses and race cars, and
fly airplanes.

In spite of the best of my youthful
efforts, those private airplanes of mine
never left the ground below, and today,
in spite of what I only prayed could be
my new best efforts, more airplanes were
sent crashing to the streets, manned by
my students and steered with hundreds
of years of ignorance and hatred, bias,
shame and mistrust. And lies.

Eventually, I stopped putting
beaded lawn chairs on my head,
gave up the chase of the human
lust for flight, and my life, though
perhaps a bit mundane and more
predictable, has almost assuredly
been improved for a lack of wearing
furniture on my head. Even as
an airplane.

Tomorrow, I will try again. Again
we will break out the tattered copies of
Reservation Blues, again we will
watch the clips of Pow-Wow Highway,
again we will flip without hope through
the photocopied, dog-eared pages of

Elsie's Business; again, again,
again.

But I know that again they will go
home to play games, they will head
out to play soccer, or in to play something
involving shooting dark-skinned criminals
on the Nintendo. And again, I will go
home and I will wonder sadly if they have
taken anything from our day. Again
I will ponder what I might have done better.
Again I will doubt alone if they might ever
stoop to pick even one single piece of broken
life from someone else's soccer field. Again
I will wonder; again, again,
again.

So tonight, with nothing in my bag but
poorly-graded narratives, my own bad
songs and someone else's borrowed dreams
to dash upon the rocks below, I will return
home, to that town below the res, and tonight
in the dark, (when my mother isn't looking)
I will fly my beaded lawn chair all about
the world and tonight, again, one final time,
I will realize what it means to be truly great at
what I do.

"February 6"

7:39 a.m.

It was just yesterday
I sat in the IEP meeting of
a boy I've known for all
of six days, like a witness
at the stand, testifying to the
great notion that this man
is not a murderer, I am certain
because we met once and
his smile was warm and he
smelled strongly of cologne.
His handshake was firm
beyond a reasonable doubt.

It was on that stand that
day that I was again reminded
of my loathing for the uterus and
penis, both indiscriminate organs
of mass conception, never
bothering to first discover whether
the vessel might become a caring
mother, whether the father can
hold down a job, or whether each
instead might seek to make some
sick profit from the product of
their sweaty, lust-filled union.

I argued my case vehemently
with the uterus-bearing parental
unit, assuming quietly that the
penis was too caught up in putting
the proverbial food on the
proverbial table to give two damns
about his wretched son. Uterus
informed me that my six-day
friend was incapable of writing,
that she had to help him. Through
livid eyes I bluntly disagreed,
told her that she was a stupid
uterus who would do much better
to encourage her son, soon to be
a full-fledged penis himself, who
had confided in me that he had
hopes of becoming a pharmacist.

I was later told by my colleagues
that after I left, uterus had informed
them that he should drop out, that
he was too stupid to get into
pharmacy school. But I would
swear under oath that he is not, and
that he will.

1:16 p.m.

We are again studying genocide.
Bosnia isn't meant to be viewed
as a vacation resort; Rwanda isn't
anybody's paradise these days. I
tell them this, as they search their
Ipods and pick at zits. A trio
of my former students arrive, half
a minute late, and quietly take their
seats, shaking my hand on the way
in. They are from the Balkans,
and they are here to share. They
are friends, three of them, amidst
hallways full of American peers who
could no sooner point to their countries
on a map than empathize with the
horrors that they have survived. They
are three friends against a country
that fought to keep them out, with only
that, a slight accent, and a taste for
pizza in common. But it's enough to
make them brothers in a world dead-
set on telling them apart.

They talk and we listen, as it
should more often be. They have
lived and they can tell us how it's
really done, how it's done when it
matters, and when you don't. There
is much I can learn from my students,

even more that they can learn from
each other.

On some, their words are scuttled
on the rocks that guard the entrance
to their ears, placed there over time
by over-zealous parents, by Bill O'Reilly
and Fox News. Don't care about
others, you are who matters. Those
who are not Capitalist Americans
deserve to die anyway. And down sinks
hope, scuttled, destroyed, into the
murky depths of oblivion. But there
are those also whose rocks are less
formidable, less engrained. For them,
the information sails by, into the ear,
blowing the foghorn and sending a
signal to the eyes, mouth and mind
who open in unison, terrified yet
needing more. The trio continues to
speak, nonplussed, shooting me glances
as if to remind me that the trigger
that operates the eyes and mouth is
in no way connected to the hands
or feet, and that the mind and the
memory are not one. They know
that they may be forgotten; we will
discuss it over pizza.

11:27 p.m.

We won tonight. As the clock
wound down our two-and-twenty
Prairiewolves breathed a long-awaited
sigh of relief, our first conference win.
For the first time all season, we had
approached an opponent with the
confidence of competitors, and the
fury of a doormat. Sometimes that's
what it takes. Young women often
never find that fury today in this
country, though many of them are
surely doormats and long overdue the
pleasure of standing up after so much
time spent on the floor. In the twenty-
point upset, our senior point guard
hurt again the foot she had broken at
the start of the season, likely ending
her career at that point. At the buzzer,
she limped quietly towards the locker
room, grinning larger than
Alice's cat, in search of ice and
another ibuprofen. Tonight, fifteen girls
and a couple coaches learned that rare
and sacred lesson, that lesson often
never learned in a land that embraces
winners, shuns losers, and
never stops competing. Tonight

we learned, praise God we learned,
that three-and-twenty can be
victorious.

"Name and Rank"

.5

How do you tell someone that the world isn't
out to get them, when it already has them by
the balls? It's a shock to learn that there are
white people who aren't privileged, but it's
also true. Sure, some of us just bitch about
our lives, like no matter what we have it will
never be enough, never be good enough for
us; like our mother forgot we wanted vanilla
instead of chocolate, so now the whole
party is ruined. But to be fair, there are an
awful lot of white folks without any parties
and without any ice cream.

I

"Will" I think he said. I've always been bad
with names. He didn't try to pretend like he
didn't want any money, but his accent was
thick, and you can usually get any information
you want for a buck, so I drug it out of him.
"Where you from?" I asked him, trying to be
casual, like I was talking to an old friend. He
stared at me, and it was then that I noticed that
his eyes had no color at all; white eggs with
piercing, shiny black yolks in them, catching
the light from the moon and from the bar signs
that hung above us on the street. "I'm from
Bosnia," he said, as though it made no difference
at first. He expected the words to mean nothing

to me, but his expression changed; he must
have seen the recognition in my features. I was
horrified, as every glaring scar on the man's face and
exposed arms took on new meaning, like a page
in a book that everyone should have read by
now, and hasn't. He smiled weakly, exposing
gums with only a few broken teeth on them, and
those eggs looked sorry for me. He almost
seemed to be saying "I am sorry to have put you
through this." But why? Why should he be
sorry? Why should he regret to inform me that
his people died because mine didn't have the
stones to act? The pity laced across those eggs was
more than I could take; he should have spit in my
face, beaten me and taken all of my money. Even
that wouldn't have been enough. He looked
down, ashamed again, but of what, I could not
imagine. Inside the bar, my friends asked where
I was. "That was Will," I tell them, with the
remnants of shock and urgency in my voice.
"He's from Bosnia." The conversation returns
to women and football in a matter of moments,
and I wonder if, in another world, Will might
have had a wife, or won the Heisman.

II

"Rick" or "Bill" it was. You remember your
boss's name because he writes your check, he
may even decide if you get one, but the guy
who needs something from you isn't important;
you forget his name and you only pretend to

listen as he tells you about his life, about the
family that left him, or that he left, or that he
wished he had. This guy had a daughter, she
lived somewhere in town and sometimes, he
said, she'd stop down and bring a sandwich.
She was poor, he said, but had an apartment. I
couldn't understand how there could be two
people in the same family, and one of them had
a roof to sleep under and the other didn't. I've
never seen an apartment so small that you couldn't
fit one more person inside of it, and hell, that
usually cuts down on the heat bill anyway. But
I guess this guy's daughter didn't see it that way,
and I suppose that's her right. Hell will be hot
enough that she won't miss the roof anymore,
but I didn't tell the old man that. After all, I bet
his daughter could remember his name, and that's
better than I can do. The guy said he had cancer,
and that it was terminal, and that it hurt. I bought
him a sandwich, which I suppose is as good a
cure for cancer as anything, because maybe it
sort of cures the part that really sucks for guys
like him, the part that reminds you that everyone
has turned their back to you, and that you're going
to die alone. Eventually, we all have to square
with that. I don't know if it's better to realize that
you're already dead in a plush, warm hospital
room, listening to your relatives argue out in the
hallway about your will, or there on the street
like that guy, with nobody there to argue, and
nothing to argue over anyway. I suspect that there is

a nifty correlation between how much valuable junk you have to will to your relatives, and how many relatives know you're dying of cancer. Maybe this guy was better off without the vultures, and just the cats like me, walking around curious and pretending to be sympathetic while we check our watches, not wanting to miss the movie, or the start of happy hour. I don't have cancer. All of my hours should be pretty damn happy.

Mike told me that he died last week. Mike is a preacher down at the city mission. Mike said his name was Bill, and I bet he's right. I wondered to myself if Bill's daughter was at the funeral. Mike said that Bill is going to heaven. I said I'd like to join him. Mike said "A-men."

III

The drop-dead gorgeous student teacher from the music department had remembered my clumsy pass at her in the copy room and apparently wasn't as offended by it as she had let on. She called me up early on Saturday morning "just to say hi." It took me awhile to figure out who she was, and to clean the taste from my mouth as I listened to her talk. Why was she awake this early? Finally, I got enough of the pieces put together in my head, and I asked if she'd like to get dinner, and she said no. But maybe coffee. I'll never understand women, but that didn't seem like the conversation to have with her, so I agreed to coffee and the next night we met up in the Haymarket. We must have talked for a couple hours; it took me a few minutes to decide she wasn't an airhead, and apparently it took her a little longer to decide I wasn't dangerous. Fair's fair. Then we went for beers at Lazlo's. On our way back, a man seated on a bench outside the coffeehouse glanced up at us, and said simply, "Can you help me?" I didn't know the girl very well, but this seemed like as good a time as any to learn the hard stuff. "Sure," I said. "Want some coffee?" My beautiful companion didn't miss a beat, and we spent the rest of the night out on the porch, drinking coffee and eating scones. His name was Karl, like the Nazi in *The Sunflower*, and he had a family, he said. Apparently, they lived in Omaha, and he needed to save enough money to get there. I didn't mention that I drive to Omaha once a week for class. All of these people who beg on the streets have family, I thought to myself, or else they are completely delusional. But if they do have family, then where the Hell is their family? Did they really raise them so poorly that now they think it's okay to give up on their own parents? We gave the man some money, and told each other we'd pray for him that night. Prayers good, money better. He was sober, and since I'm judgmental, that mattered to me. I hope he got to Omaha. The pretty girl and I dated for a few more weeks, then found other things to do. We still talk from time to time, but typically not about Karl.

IV

He said his name was Samuel, and maybe it really was. He stumbled toward me the way I used to stumble off the party bus and back into the fraternity when I was busy learning nothing about anything and everything about nothing back in college. He was hammered, but so was I, so it took me a little longer than it should have to come to realize it.

"I have something for you," he told me, and I bristled like a cornered porcupine. At the time I was working the door at a local public house and I wasn't afraid of him or anyone else, except for the fact that he scared the shit out of me. But it wasn't a fist and a shot at my wallet that he had in mind to give to me. He had noticed the ornate beaded bone choker around my neck, the one I used to brag about having been made up on the res. And it really was, just not for me. Another piece of white jewelry, another example of a lost soul blindly appropriating someone else's culture because he has none of his own.

"Do you like Indians?" Samuel asked me, slyly. This was a no-brainer, especially since he was one, so I nodded. "Sure."

"Toksa," he said to me with a sweeping bow. I looked at him funny, and he reared his head back like he was eighteen hands high and stared down his nose at me, enunciating carefully so that the well-dressed ignoramus could understand what he was saying.

"Dok-shuh" he said again and again. "The 'T' makes a 'D' and it's a farewell. It means that we're brothers, we're all related. I thought about that; was I related to this man, and if so, would I get any of his inheritance? I should probably go to the hospital when he started to die, just in case.

"Mitakuye Oyasin," I replied to him. He was Lakota, and he knew what I was saying. "So brother," he began with that sly look on his face again, his eyes watering strongly, as though I was his only brother in the world, "got a couple bucks?" We finished getting drunk together.

Toksa. I kept it, and I used it when talking to my best Indian friend, right up until the time she found out that I was a Christian and accused me of trying to steal her soul. I didn't want her stupid soul, and if she'd read her damn history, she'd have known that the "Christians" that she hated so much didn't even think she had one because she wasn't white. But I knew she did; I know that we all do. That wasn't enough for her. Two hundred years of ingrained hatred, a spell in a boarding school, and most likely a lifetime of horrible names, and worse than that, presumptions, had left her so damaged that there was no future for me in her life as a follower of Christ, even if

I was the first one she'd ever really met. So she sits in her air-conditioned office in Tucson, and I remain in Lincoln, and each of us spend our days writing what we think are clever things about life, our life, and love and race and history, our history, and somewhere else, my brother Samuel is still cold, and still tired, and still hungry.

IV.5

I remember being a tiny kid, and my mother tucking me in every night. Some nights she read to me about the mighty Aslan and how he conquered Narnia, and some nights she reminded me that sneetches are sneetches, and no kind of sneetch is the best on the beaches. And she was right. For all her privilege and pale skin, she's still going to die of cancer soon. Nobody cares if you're chocolate or if you're vanilla when you're dying. You could even be cherry. Some of us have more vultures than others, just like some of us have more stuff, but really, sneethes are sneetches, and in the end I guess all we can hope for is that we're the kind of sneetch that has a house to live in, and food and maybe another sneetch or two to share it with. I think that was the point of the story about Aslan, too, but anymore, I can't seem to remember for sure.

"America the Beautiful"

The land of the free was stolen from the brave;
we live here, and yes, we have a problem with that.
Two hundred years of violence, of culture trampled
under hooves, can not, will not, ever be atoned for.

One nation under God, just as long as it's my god, just
so long as that god is the one that worships me.
Sacrifice your conscience at the altar of ambition,
steal what you can not have, murder when it suits you,
bulldoze another's sacred place, park there and pray,
one nation under God.

If you believe in Jesus then you can't believe in this;
you can't preach peace from behind the counter at a
Starbucks, you can't go to work at the Bureau of
Caucasian Affairs and then pass the pipe to the stock
boy in aisle four.

If you believe in the Holy Spirit then this is not the
land for you; what happened to the Spirit of Brotherly
Love? What part of our own spirits are Holy now that
we live in a world where only cheaters and thieves
can survive?

So pledge allegiance to the latest flag to fly over this
land, and know that it won't be the last, for the blood
of the red is not our blood. Ours stains the white until
only the blue from our tears remains. Glory! Glory!
Halleluiah! We unholy pilgrims must lay down the

sword, hit our knees and pray that we, with liberty and justice for all, may be forgiven.

"Let Me Tell You What I'm Made Of"

When I was little, I fell in the driveway of my maternal grandparent's farm, now part of Lincoln, Nebraska. My bare knee met the broken shards of brick that composed the beaten path, and I began bleeding streams of perfect red, running like my tears down my leg and pooling in my sock.

I am German and I am English. Mortal enemies collide within every artery and vein.

I am no/sixteenths Sioux,
> but I would be honored if the French thought that I, too, was responsible for the fall of man.

I am no/sixteenths Navajo,
> but my cousin drove truck for them some years ago.

I am no/sixteenths Cherokee,
> and I must be the only damn person in the country who isn't.

I am no/sixteenths Teton,
> but my dad took me camping there when I was little. I would play on the rocks with my G.I. Joes. The 7th Cavalry always lost.

I am no/sixteenths Seminole,
> but I saw they lost to Clemson last week at home.

The mortal red that runs within me, courses through me like the angry tides of time, like the rivers through the gullies, composed of mighty rains once sent to wipe away mankind. It pulses and it surges, as I run inside, crying, begging mother to remove the shards.

Every man, his blood the best, every man unites to do battle with his neighbor, with his bastard son. There is no amount of sixteenths that can satisfy man's lust for blood, fulfill his ambitions, and leave the world perfect, sixteen/sixteenths full of healthy, wet redness.

Mother, mother, what have we become?

"The Start of Something Good"

I was sitting in the Mill South for over half an hour, the little girl behind me gently flicking her muffin crumbs upon my sandaled feet as she dined, when I realized that my pants were not buttoned.

People are bleak and ugly, unless you step inside of them and see the light. I remember that my father's favorite part of driving that cramped orange Honda Civic to the Black Hills was passing through the reservation. The aluminum siding on the gas station would catch the sun and point a beam upon the HUD houses, point another one right at my heart, and make me wonder why I ever did my math homework at all, while elsewhere people danced and sang and beat their drum without fear of geometric murder. My father saw inside the reservation, saw that it was beautiful. He knew what was in there and he loved it.

The little girl is named Amani, and she is two years old. She graduated from the muffin and has moved on to a cookie. Having finished that part of the cookie that she wanted to eat, she is asking me about *Still Life Moving*, the book I'm reading. Someday she will like it too, and we will discuss it over muffins.

And cookies.

Dad would have liked to stop short of the Black Hills and just vacation on the res, take a hike in the woods, maybe go see Don sundance if the time was right. It was me who always needed the caves and the alligators and the water slide at the Ramada Inn. The trigonometry of youth, I needed the math, needed a brochure from someplace sterilized to show my friends at recess, as we compared our weekend exploits and competed to see who could piss the farthest through the chain link fence. I needed the sum to equal more than the whole, the Indians not counting for much amongst my youthful cohorts, history never being any of our strong suit.

I wonder what my father will tell Amani when he meets her; I wonder what she'll tell him while she's eating her muffin, the crumbs falling softly on his muddy hiking boots. I wonder if the two of them will even remember me as they begin to plan a holiday at Bill's house, stopping by the reservation on the way to watch Don dance and beat the sacred drum, chanting softly just to them.

Hey-uh, hey-ah, hey.

 Mark Gudgel is an English teacher at Lincoln Southwest High School who has been blessed with having extraordinary students and, on most days, enough passion and compassion to counteract his vast array of deficiencies. Mark grew up in Valentine, Nebraska, nine miles south of the Rosebud Reservation, and spent many weekends with his parents on the Rosebud, the Pine Ridge, and in the Black Hills. Mark is a graduate of the University of Nebraska-Lincoln and is presently completing a master's degree in Biblical Theology at Grace University in Omaha. His work in the classroom has earned him recognition in the field of Holocaust education, though most importantly, it has given him the opportunity to continue working with the youth of America. *No/sixteenths* is Mark's first full-length book of poetry, and was written over a period of several years, between early college and the present. His second book, *Contempt Issues*, is expected to be in available in 2010.

PHOTO CREDIT: Khara Plicanic/Kabloom Studios

"Mark Gudgel suffers from an illness far in excess of typical white guilt. It is that near-suicidal self-assault of historical truth. All the euphemistic prisms thorough which the harsh light of time is bent into glow-in-the-dark velvet paintings, the brilliant spectra of Navaho weavings, or carved cedar cigar-store totems he redirects back upon itself - tying himself and all of us together in a knot of all our shame and lies. So as it is true for our Native sisters and brothers, reading this book our continent becomes a wasteland in which there are no rest stops nor places to hide. One must stand on one's feet reading this book, as one stands up in the presence of courage – to honor it and because it frightens us and we make ready to flee. These poems are daymares with the small of blood still fresh in them. Drums and gunshots fill our every breath. There are two choices here: to read these poems and weep, or to deny them and go back to sleep."

- Greg Kuzma

"If you are a reader with thin skin, you might not want to pursue these poems and stories. They pack a variety of punches – some social, others political, many religious. More than a few combine the punches, and the upshot is a challenging laying-out of the writer's convictions. I was especially struck by "Quiet Summer's Afternoon" and "America the Beautiful." Sneak a peek at these, if you dare, to test the thickness of the skin. Then permit your own audacity to take you wherever it chooses to go."

- William Kloefkorn

"Mark Gudgel's *no/sixteenths* marks the arrival of a young and exciting poet whose fierce eye explodes historical and current events. In his ambitious first book, Gudgel takes on race, class, and identity to explore the tragic events shaping our world – from the Holocaust to the genocide in Darfur to the atrocities committed against the Native American Peoples in the United States. "Fear defines my people," writes Gudgel, who, as a result, "are always hungry." Such irony cuts deep in poems that question humanity's lust for violence and power. All the while, Gudgel guides his readers with a generosity of spirit informed by his life as a teacher and religious scholar. "Tomorrow, I will try again," writes Gudgel, reminding us that we are not along as we begin our slow crawl toward hope."

- Hadara Bar-Nadav

"*no/sixteenths* is not a book to be read and put aside. It begs to be studied, scribbled in, dog eared and discussed. The secret to writing good poetry is letting the poem decide when to stop, and this author has an uncanny sense about that. Gudgel is a shape shifter; part archaeologist, part anthropologist, and dead serious about the theological paradoxes of mankind. He hauls his readers relentlessly into classrooms, churches, along alleys, across the rez, and down to the depths of the souls some of us have forgotten we have; yet somehow manages to bring us safely home."

- Lyn Messersmith

www.ingramcontent.com/pod-product-compliance
Lightning Source LLC
Chambersburg PA
CBHW031208090426
42736CB00009B/827